rockschool®

Male Vocals
Grade 6

*Performance pieces, technical exercises and in-depth guidance
for Rockschool examinations*

Acknowledgements

Published by Rockschool Ltd. © 2014 under license from Music Sales Ltd.
Catalogue Number RSK091414
ISBN: 978-1-908920-64-5

AUDIO
Backing tracks produced by Music Sales Limited
Supporting test backing tracks recorded by Jon Musgrave, Jon Bishop and Duncan Jordan
Supporting test vocals recorded by Duncan Jordan
Supporting tests mixed at Langlei Studios by Duncan Jordan
Mastered by Duncan Jordan

MUSICIANS
Neal Andrews, Lucie Burns (Lazy Hammock), Jodie Davies,Tenisha Edwards, Noam Lederman,
Beth Loates-Taylor, Dave Marks, Salena Mastroianni, Paul Miro, Ryan Moore, Jon Musgrave,
Chris Smart, Ross Stanley, T-Jay, Stacy Taylor, Daniel Walker

PUBLISHING
Compiled and edited by James Uings, Simon Troup, Stephen Lawson and Stuart Slater
Internal design and layout by Simon and Jennie Troup, Digital Music Art
Cover designed by Philip Millard, Philip Millard Design
Fact Files written by Stephen Lawson, Owen Bailey and Michael Leonard
Additional proofing by Chris Bird, Ronan Macdonald, Jonathan Preiss and Becky Baldwin
Cover photography © Eugene Adebari / Rex Features
Full transcriptions by Music Sales Ltd.

SYLLABUS
Vocal specialists: Martin Hibbert and Eva Brandt
Additional Consultation: Emily Nash, Stuart Slater and Sarah Page
Supporting Tests Composition: Martin Hibbert, James Uings, Jon Musgrave, Jodie Davies,
Ryan Moore, Chris Hawkins, Jonathan Preiss

PRINTING
Printed and bound in the United Kingdom by Caligraving Ltd.
Media hosting by Dropcards

DISTRIBUTION
Exclusive Distributors: Music Sales Ltd.

CONTACTING ROCKSCHOOL
www.rockschool.co.uk
Telephone: +44 (0)845 460 4747
Fax: +44 (0)845 460 1960

Table of Contents

Introductions & Information

Page

Rockschool Grade Pieces

Page

Technical Exercises

Page

Supporting Tests

Page

Additional Information

Page

Welcome to Rockschool Male Vocals Grade 6

Welcome to the Rockschool Male Vocals Grade 6 pack. This book and accompanying download card contain everything you need to sing at this grade.

Vocals Exams

At each grade you have the option of taking one of two different types of examination:

- **Grade Exam:** a Grade Exam is a mixture of music performances, technical work and tests. You prepare three pieces (two of which may be Free Choice Pieces) and the contents of the Technical Exercise section. This accounts for 75% of the exam marks. The other 25% consists of: a Quick Study Piece (10%), two Ear Tests (10%), and finally you will be asked five General Musicianship Questions (5%). The pass mark is 60%.

- **Performance Certificate:** in a Performance Certificate you sing five pieces. Up to three of these can be Free Choice Pieces. Each song is marked out of 20 and the pass mark is 60%.

Book Contents

The book is divided into a number of sections. These are:

- **Exam Pieces:** in this book you will find six well-known pieces of Grade 6 standard. Each song is preceded by a Fact File detailing information about the original recording, the artist who sang on it and some recommended listening if you wish to research the artist further.

- **Piano and guitar notation:** every exam piece is printed with a piano part and guitar chords. Both are a representation of the overall band arrangement. These have been included to assist you with your practice should you wish to use a piano and/or guitar for accompaniment. In your exam you must perform to the backing tracks provided.

- **Vocal score:** in addition to the piano/vocal/guitar arrangement there is also a separate vocal-only score to allow you to view the vocal part on a single sheet of paper.

- **Technical Exercises:** there are a range of technical exercises in this grade. Some are notated in full, and some give a range of starting notes.

- **Supporting Tests and General Musicianship Questions:** in Vocals Grade 6 there are three supporting tests – a Quick Study Piece, two Ear Tests and a set of General Musicianship Questions (GMQs) asked at the end of each exam. Examples of the types of tests likely to appear in the exam are printed in this book.

- **General Information:** finally, you will find information on exam procedures, including online examination entry, marking schemes, information on Free Choice Pieces and improvisation requirements for each grade.

Audio

Each song in Vocals Grade 6 has an audio track that can be downloaded via the download card that comes with the book. This is a backing track with the vocal taken off so you can sing along with the band. The backing tracks should be used in examinations. There are also audio examples of the supporting tests printed in the book.

The audio files are supplied in MP3 format, the most widely compatible audio format in common usage – MP3s will likely be familiar to anyone with a computer, iPod, smartphone or similar device. Once downloaded you will be able to play them on any compatible device; we hope that you find this extra versatility useful.

Download cards

Download cards are easy to use – simply go to *www.dropcards.com/rsvocals* and type in the code on the back of your card. It's best to do this somewhere with a good connection, to ensure that the download is uninterrupted. If you have any problems with your download, you should be able to resolve them at *www.dropcards.com/help*.

Supporting Test Notation

The supporting tests in this book and its corresponding exam are written one octave higher than they sound. This is common practice and avoids excessive use of ledger notes.

We hope you enjoy using this book. You can find further details about Rockschool's Vocals and other instrumental syllabuses on our website: *www.rockschool.co.uk*.

SONG TITLE: AIN'T NO SUNSHINE
ALBUM: JUST AS I AM
RELEASED: 1971
LABEL: SUSSEX RECORDS
GENRE: SOUL

PERSONNEL: BILL WITHERS (VOX)
STEPHEN STILLS (GTR)
DONALD DUNN (BASS)
AL JACKSON (DRUMS)

UK CHART PEAK: 40
US CHART PEAK: 3

Slow rock-blues feel (♩ = 80)

1. Ain't no sun - shine when she's

BACKGROUND INFO

'Ain't No Sunshine' is classic 1970s soul and the song that pushed Bill Withers to stardom. It's from his debut album, *Just As I Am*, recorded when Withers was already in his 30s.

THE BIGGER PICTURE

William Harrison 'Bill' Withers Jr was born in 1938 in West Virginia, USA. From 18 years of age, Withers served nine years in the US Navy before launching his musical career. While on downtime during his navy call of duty, he honed his songwriting, guitar playing and singing. When discharged, Withers relocated to Los Angeles to forge a career in music. In 1970, he was signed by Sussex Records owner Clarence Avant. Sussex booked former Stax Records stalwart Booker T Jones as producer, even though Sussex was not a major label – to bring in such stellar musicians to back Withers was testament to the singer's promise. Withers's inspiration for this song, in his own words, seems bizarre. He said, "I was watching a movie called *Days Of Wine And Roses* [1962] with Lee Remick and Jack Lemmon. They were both alcoholics who were alternately weak and strong. It's like going back for seconds on rat poison. Sometimes you miss things that weren't particularly good for you. It's just something that crossed my mind from watching that movie, and probably something else that happened in my life that I'm not aware of." So, it's a bittersweet lyric. 'Ain't No Sunshine' won a Grammy in 1972 for Best R&B Song after selling over a million copies.

NOTES

Withers's repeated "I know, I know, I know, I know…" lines were recorded when he was still trying to complete his lyrics. But producer Booker T Jones insisted he should keep these in the final mix. The song's melancholic appeal is special. 'Ain't No Sunshine' is a song of mostly minor chords (only one major, a G). It's also a rarity in that it begins with singing before any instrumentation.

RECOMMENDED LISTENING

This classic is much-covered. The Jackson 5, Paul McCartney, Paul Weller, Sting, Eva Cassidy and even Zakk Wylde have all covered 'Ain't No Sunshine'. Bill Withers's later smash 'Lovely Day' echoes the repeat-lyric on a more upbeat funkier hit. 'Just The Two Of Us' is another Withers-written classic you can listen to for comparison. His hit cover of 'Lean On Me' is also great study for vocal phrasing.

Ain't No Sunshine

Bill Withers
Words & Music by Bill Withers

SONG TITLE: COUNTING STARS
ALBUM: NATIVE
RELEASED: 2013
LABEL: INTERSCOPE
GENRE: POP

PERSONNEL: RYAN TEDDER (VOX+KEYS)
ZACH FILKINS (GTR)
DREW BROWN (VARIOUS)
EDDIE FISHER (DRUMS)

UK CHART PEAK: 1
US CHART PEAK: 24

BACKGROUND INFO

'Counting Stars' was the first single from OneRepublic's third studio album, *Native*.

THE BIGGER PICTURE

OneRepublic formed in Los Angeles circa 2003 after frontman Ryan Tedder (vocals, keys) persuaded his former school bandmate Zach Filkins (guitar) to join him in California. Tedder had worked in the music industry since college, first as an intern working on demos at Dreamworks Records, Nashville, then as an apprentice to R'n'B/hip hop producer Timbaland, who also helped Tedder with his own development as a music artist. OneRepublic – "a rock band that has an obsession with pop melodies", according to Tedder – were signed to Columbia Records and spent two and a half years working on their debut album. However, just months before the record's scheduled release date, the band were dropped by their label. Fortunately, OneRepublic were gaining fans on MySpace. "We blew up out of nowhere," said Tedder. OneRepublic were hot property, and offers from record companies flooded in. In the end, the band decided to sign with a subsidiary of Interscope, represented by Tedder's former employer, Timbaland. A Timbaland remix of the group's single 'Apologize' featured on the producer's own album *Shock Value* (2007) and broke OneRepublic to a wider audience.

NOTES

According to Billboard.com, 'Counting Stars' was an even bigger seller than OneRepublic's once ubiquitous debut single, 'Apologize'. Although frontman Ryan Tedder is a professional songwriter for other artists ('Bleeding Love' by Leona Lewis is one of his bigger hits), his goal for OneRepublic isn't necessarily to write a Number 1, especially if that means pandering to popular tastes. He told Billboard, "If everybody else sings about sex and love and lust and money, then somebody's gotta be singing about life and faith and hope… I'd rather have a song that peaks at Number 15 that's meaningful and embedded in the cultural framework we live in than a Number 1 song that explodes for five seconds, becomes the dance hit of the summer, then goes away."

RECOMMENDED LISTENING

OneRepublic's debut album may have had a troubled launch, but it stands as the best testimony to the band's abilities and Tedder's songwriting.

Counting Stars

OneRepublic

Words & Music by Ryan Tedder

Late-ly I been,_ I been los-ing sleep_ dream-ing a-bout_ the things that we could be. But ba-by, I been,_ I been pray-in' hard,_ said no more count-ing dol-lars we'll be count-ing stars. Yeah, we'll be count-ing stars._

1. I see this

life like a swing-ing vine,___ swing my heart a-cross the line.___ In my face is flash-ing signs,___

seek it out and ye shall find.___ Old, but I'm not that old. Young, but I'm not that bold. And

Take that mon-ey watch it burn. Sink in the ri-ver, the les - sons I learned.

Take that mon-ey watch it burn. Sink in the ri-ver, the les - sons I learned.

Take that mon-ey watch it burn. Sink in the ri-ver, the les - sons I learned.

Ev - 'ry - thing that kills me makes me feel a - live.

SONG TITLE: I CAN'T QUIT YOU BABY
ALBUM: LED ZEPPELIN
RELEASED: 1969
LABEL: ATLANTIC
GENRE: BLUES ROCK

PERSONNEL: ROBERT PLANT (VOX)
JIMMY PAGE (GUITAR)
JOHN PAUL JONES (BASS)
JOHN BONHAM (DRUMS)

UK CHART PEAK: N/A
US CHART PEAK: N/A

BACKGROUND INFO

'I Can't Quit You Baby' is from Led Zeppelin's self-titled debut album. It wasn't a hit *per se* as, in the UK, Led Zeppelin didn't release singles. But the album hit Number 6 in the UK and Number 10 in the US.

THE BIGGER PICTURE

Led Zeppelin were formed in London in 1968 by ex-Yardbird/session guitarist Jimmy Page, session bassist John Paul Jones, and Robert Plant and John Bonham from midlands group The Band Of Joy. At first, they were called The New Yardbirds as the 'old' Yardbirds still had a few weeks' gig contracts to honour in Scandinavia. With contracts fulfilled, the new band needed a new name. It was The Who's drummer Keith Moon and bassist John Entwistle who suggested that a supergroup containing themselves, Jimmy Page and Jeff Beck would go down like a "lead balloon", an idiom for disastrous results. Balloon was swapped for Zeppelin and the 'led' spelling was to stop it being mispronounced 'leed'. Led Zeppelin's debut album was recorded in just 36 hours. Page said, "It's got overdubs on it, but the original tracks are live." And with a reported bill of just £1,782, *Led Zeppelin* is surely one of the most profitable rock albums ever recorded. Led Zeppelin and their manager funded all the album's recording, before signing to Atlantic Records. Once Atlantic were bowled over by the completed album tapes, Zeppelin demanded total control of all music released (no singles!), artwork and producers (Page plus his chosen engineers), and secured a bigger royalty rate than even The Beatles.

NOTES

Although originally credited to the four Zeppelin members, 'I Can't Quit You Baby' was written by blues songwriting legend Willie Dixon and first recorded by Otis Rush in 1956. In the 1980s, Dixon sued Led Zeppelin. The case was settled out of court, with Dixon getting a credit and share of Zeppelin's by-then massive royalties. Dixon also secured a co-credit for 'Whole Lotta Love' from *Led Zeppelin II*.

RECOMMENDED LISTENING

Listen to the Otis Rush original release to compare. For other examples of Led Zeppelin 'reworking' classic blues, listen to 'Whole Lotta Love' (originally recorded in 1963 by Muddy Waters as 'You Need Love', and also written by Dixon) and 'When The Levee Breaks' on *Led Zeppelin IV* (originally by Kansas Joe McCoy and Memphis Minnie, from 1929).

I Can't Quit You Baby

Led Zeppelin

Words & Music by Willie Dixon

Oh!_____

Oh!__

Instrumental adlib

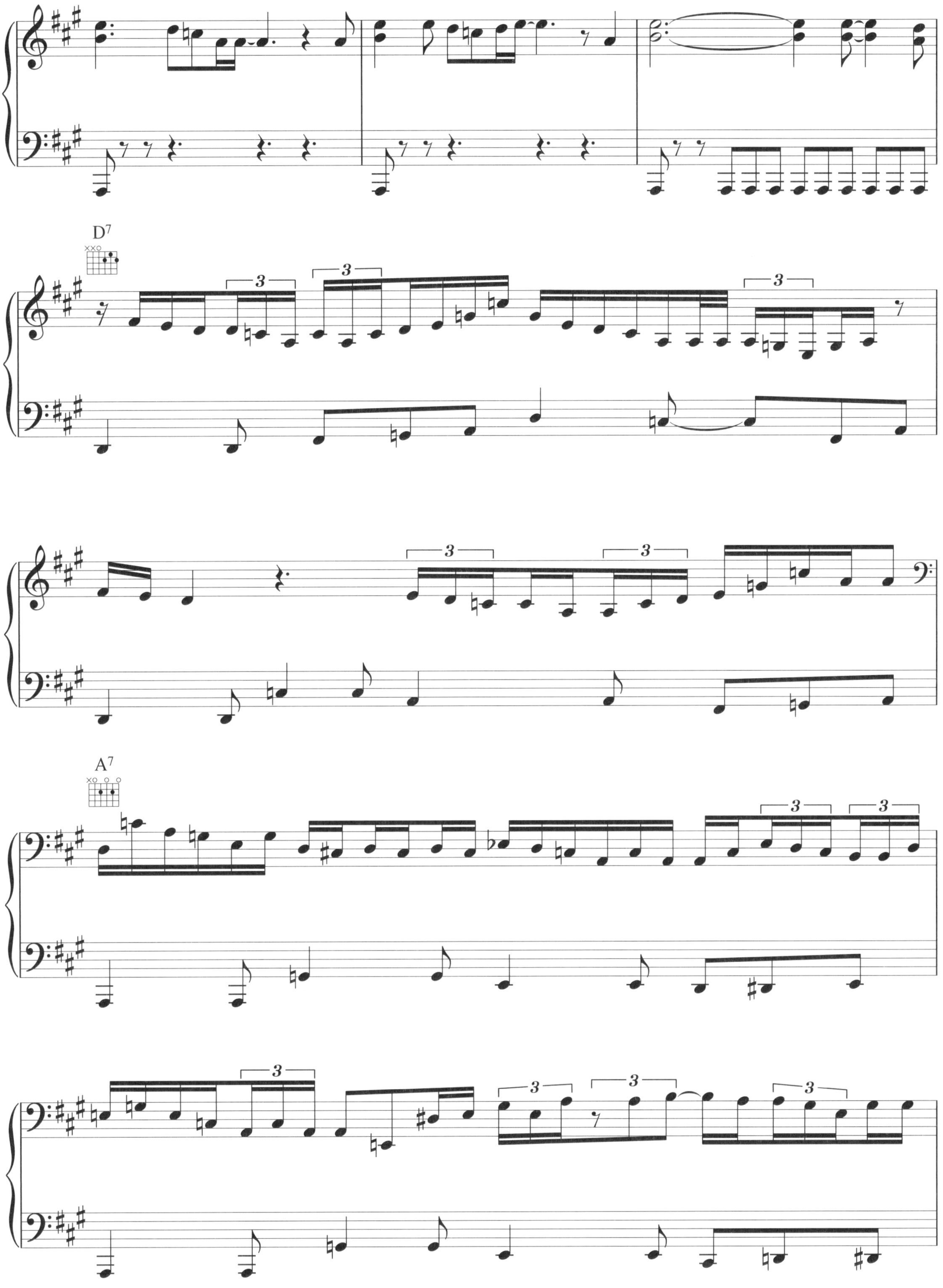
D7
A7

3. When you hear me moan-ing and groan-ing babe you know it hurts me deep down

in-side. Oh,

SONG TITLE: JEALOUSY
ALBUM: ECHOES
RELEASED: 2011
LABEL: RCA
GENRE: POP

PERSONNEL: WILL YOUNG (VOX)

UK CHART PEAK: 5
US CHART PEAK: N/A

BACKGROUND INFO

'Jealousy' was the first single released from Will Young's fifth studio album, *Echoes*. It was his first Top 10 hit since 2008's 'Changes'.

THE BIGGER PICTURE

Will Young was born in Wokingham, Berkshire in 1979. Young was four years old when he first trod the boards, appearing as a fir tree (with one spoken line of dialogue) in a school play. Later, he was head chorister of his preparatory school choir and took piano lessons. While attending boarding school, Young appeared in several plays but was more interested in sports than music, aspiring to one day run the 400 metres at the Olympics. After resitting his A Levels, Young read Politics at the University of Exeter and joined a theatre group, where he landed the lead role in *Oklahoma!* He did work experience at Sony Records and, having decided to make a go of performing, enrolled at the Arts Educational Schools in London to polish his act. Young successfully auditioned for a boy band, but the group failed to make any impact and disbanded. His break came in 2001, when he took part in the television talent contest *Pop Idol*, which he won in 2002. His debut single 'Anything Is Possible' was the first of four

Number 1 songs in the UK. Of his five studio albums, three have been Number 1s and two have gone to Number 2 in the British album charts.

NOTES

Will Young became a regular on the British charts thanks to a musical style that leant towards balladry and inoffensive 'shop music'. For his fifth studio album, he turned to producer Richard X to help him realise a long-held aim: to release an album of edgier, electronic material. Young told Billboard, "[*Echoes*] is an album I've wanted to do for about five years, and I've been waiting like a tiger, ready to pounce. You have to evolve as a pop artist. It's like being a magician: if you show all your best hands at the beginning, you have nothing left to reveal." Richard X was joined by several other producer and writers on Echoes. 'Jealousy' was one of several tracks co-written by Young and electronic duo Kish Mauve.

RECOMMENDED LISTENING

If you like the more electronic direction of 'Jealousy' then Echoes is worth a listen. To hear all of Young's biggest tracks – 'shop music', ballads and all – try *The Essential Will Young* (2013).

Jealousy

Will Young

Words & Music by Will Young, James Eliot & Jemima Stilwell

know, hey,___ I ought to leave the young thing a - lone,___ but ain't no sun - shine when she's

D.S. al Coda

gone.___ Ain't no sun - shine when she's

⊕ Coda

An - y - time___ she goes a - way.

Counting Stars

OneRepublic

Words & Music by Ryan Tedder

♩ = 120

Late - ly I been, I been los - ing sleep dream - ing a - bout the things that we could be. But ba - by, I been, I been pray - in' hard, said no more count - ing dol - lars we'll be count - ing stars. Yeah, we'll be count - ing stars.

1. I see this life like a swing - ing vine, swing my heart a - cross the line. In my face is flash - ing signs, seek it out and ye shall find. Old, but I'm not that old. Young, but I'm not that bold. And I don't think the world is sold, I'm just do - ing what we're told. I feel some - thing so right do - ing the wrong thing. And I feel some - thing so wrong do - ing the right thing.

I could - n't lie, could - n't lie, could - n't lie; ev - 'ry - thing that kills me makes me feel a - live.
I could - n't lie, could - n't lie, could - n't lie; ev - 'ry - thing that drowns me makes me wan - na fly.

Late - ly I been, I been los - ing sleep dream - ing a - bout the things that we could be. But ba - by, I been, I been pray - in' hard, said no more count - ing dol - lars we'll be count - ing stars. Late - ly I been, I been los - ing sleep dream - ing a - bout the things that we could be. But ba - by, I been,

I know you are my one de - sire._____ Oh!_____ Oh!_____

24

3. When you hear me moan-ing and groan - ing babe   you know it hurts me deep down__

__ in - side.   Oh,_____

__ when you hear me moan - ing and groan-ing babe,   you know it hurts me deep____ down in -

-side.   Oh!_____

When you hear me hol-ler ba - by,   you_____ know you're my one__ de - sire._____

Yes   you are.____   oh!

Jealousy

Will Young

Words & Music by Will Young, James Eliot & Jemima Stilwell

Sex On Fire

Kings of Leon

Words & Music by Caleb Followill, Nathan Followill,
Jared Followill & Matthew Followill

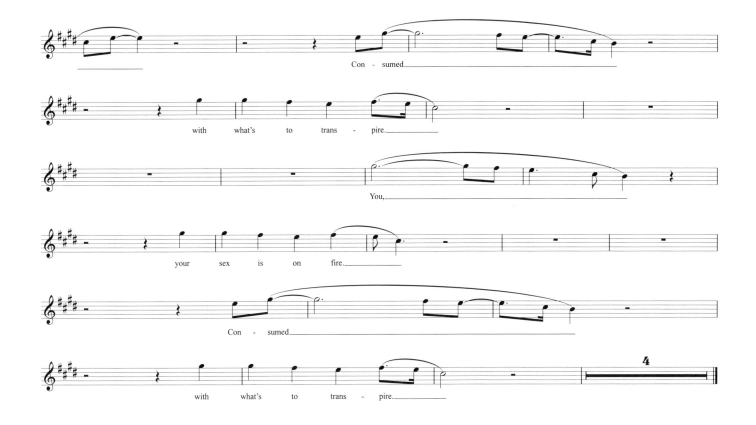

Con - sumed

with   what's   to   trans - pire.

You,

your   sex   is   on   fire.

Con - sumed

with   what's   to   trans - pire.

Man In The Mirror

Michael Jackson

Words & Music by Glen Ballard & Siedah Garrett

© Copyright 1987 Yellow Brick Road Music, USA/Universal Music Corporation/Arlovol Music.
Universal/MCA Music Limited/BMG Rights Management (UK) Limited.
All Rights Reserved. International Copyright Secured.

I Can't Quit You Baby

Led Zeppelin
Words & Music by Willie Dixon

Ain't No Sunshine

Bill Withers

Words & Music by Bill Withers

Slow rock-blues feel (♩ = 80)

1. Ain't no sun - shine when she's gone. It's not warm__ when__ she's a - way.

Ain't no sun - shine when she's gone,__ and she's al - ways gone too long an - y - time__ she goes a - way.

2. Won - der this__ time where she's gone, won - der if__ she's__ gone to
gone, on - ly dark - ness__ ev - 'ry

stay.⎫
day.⎭ Ain't no sun - shine when she's gone,__ and this house just ain't no

To Coda ⊕

home an - y - time__ she goes a - way. And I know, I know, I know,__ I know,

I know, I know, I know,__ I know,__ I know I know, I know,__ I know, I know, I know,

__ I know, I know, I know, I know,__ I know, I know, I know, I know,__ I know, I know, I

SONG TITLE: MAN IN THE MIRROR
ALBUM: BAD
RELEASED: 1988
LABEL: EPIC
GENRE: POP

PERSONNEL: MICHAEL JACKSON (VOX)
DANN HUFF (GUITAR)
GREG PHILLINGANES (KEYS)
GLEN BALLARD (SYNTH)
RANDY KERBER (SYNTH)

UK CHART PEAK: 2
US CHART PEAK: 1

BACKGROUND INFO

'Man In The Mirror' was the fourth single from Michael Jackson's seventh solo album, *Bad*.

THE BIGGER PICTURE

Michael Jackson was born in Gary, Indiana in 1958. As a child, he was encouraged by his father Joe to perform in a band with his brothers. The Jackson 5 toured America's mid west throughout the mid 1960s, supporting the major soul and R&B acts of the day. Jackson's father was a strict disciplinarian whose abuse affected the singer all his life. As an adult, Jackson was equivocal about his father's treatment of him, admitting it amounted to abuse but at the same time acknowledging Jackson Sr's part in his success. The Jackson 5 signed to Motown in 1969 and saw their first four singles reach Number 1 on the American singles chart. Jackson soon emerged as the group's frontman, with his athletic dance moves (inspired by James Brown) and magnetic stage presence. His first solo album with Motown, *Got To Be There*, was released in 1972 and followed by three more while Michael remained a member of The Jackson 5. His solo career as an adult began properly when he signed to Epic Records and released his album *Off The Wall* (1979). This impressive debut teamed Jackson up with producer/arranger Quincy Jones and some of the best session musicians on the scene. It was followed in the 1980s by *Thriller* and *Bad*, as Michael Jackson turned from star of The Jacksons to superstar in his own right. He died in 2009 from an overdose of intravenous sedative. His doctor was charged with manslaughter and served half of a four-year sentence for delivering the lethal dose.

NOTES

'Man In The Mirror' was one of seven singles released from the album *Bad*. It was written by Glen Ballard, who played synth on the record, and Siedah Garrett, who sang backing vocals. Glen Ballard is best known for his work as co-writer and producer of Alanis Morissette's hit album *Jagged Little Pill* (1995). Siedah Garrett also sang a duet with Jackson, 'I Just Can't Stop Loving You', which also featured on *Bad* and was the first single released from the album.

RECOMMENDED LISTENING

Michael Jackson's first three albums with Epic Records – *Off The Wall* (1979), *Thriller* (1982) and *Bad* (1987) – represent the pinnacle of his artistry and should form a part of any pop collection.

Man In The Mirror

Michael Jackson
Words & Music by Glen Ballard & Siedah Garrett

SONG TITLE: SEX ON FIRE

ALBUM: ONLY BY THE NIGHT

RELEASED: 2008

LABEL: RCA/VICTOR

GENRE: ROCK

PERSONNEL: CALEB FOLLOWILL (VOX+GTR)

NATHAN FOLLOWILL (DRUMS)

JARED FOLLOWILL (BASS)

MATTHEW FOLLOWILL (GTR)

UK CHART PEAK: 1

US CHART PEAK: 56

BACKGROUND INFO

'Sex On Fire' was the first single from Kings Of Leon's fourth album, *Only By The Night*.

THE BIGGER PICTURE

Brothers Caleb, Jared and Nathan Followill, sons of a travelling preacher, grew up in the southern states of the US before moving to Nashville, "kidnapping" their cousin Matthew to play lead guitar and embracing the rock 'n' roll lifestyle. When they arrived with their debut, 2001's *Youth & Young Manhood*, Kings Of Leon were hailed as the 'southern Strokes' on account of their guitar-led garage rock sound, but their inspirations were very different. Blending the southern rock of bands such as Lynyrd Skynyrd and the Allman Brothers with pop-rock craft, their brand of boogie rock won them plaudits among critics, particularly abroad, with *NME* describing *Youth…* as one of the best debuts of the last decade. Their next two albums took their sound in more experimental directions and built a fanbase in Europe. The band returned to the US to tour with U2, whose finely-honed arena rock must have made an impression viewed from close quarters, as Kings Of Leon's fourth album, 2008's *Only By The Night*, was injected with an anthemic quality that made them global superstars.

NOTES

Recorded in Nashville's Blackbird Studio in 2008, 'Sex On Fire' nearly never made it to tape: according to *Sound On Sound* magazine, singer Caleb needed "some coaxing to convince him the song was worth doing" and further persuasion to overdub his vocals. Producer Jacquire King said: "Everyone felt it was a great melody and song, and the band already has a reputation for singing about sex, so we encouraged him as much as we could. In any case, rock 'n' roll has always been fairly explicit." When he wrote the song, Caleb was suffering from a shoulder injury that made playing the guitar difficult, which perhaps explains how it's based on a straightforward motif picked on two strings. Despite 'Sex On Fire''s huge success, Caleb still seems nonplussed about it. He told *Guitar World*: "We've written songs about life and death and religion and all these important things… and then our first big hit is about your sex being on fire… They like this song, so God bless 'em."

RECOMMENDED LISTENING

Kings Of Leon's musical transformation from garage-rockers to rock superstars is best witnessed album-by-album, but for an introduction, try *Aha Shake Heartbreak* (2004).

Sex On Fire

Kings of Leon

Words & Music by Caleb Followill, Nathan Followill,
Jared Followill & Matthew Followill

1. Lay where you're lay -

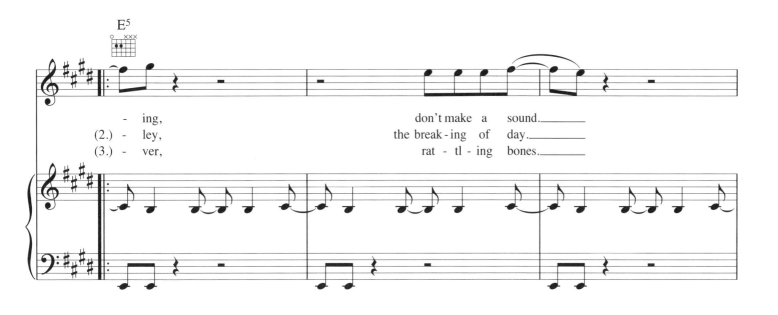

the kid - die like play,_____ it has peo - ple talk -
the knuck-les are pale,_____ feels like you're dy -
if it's just to - night,_____ oh, it's still the great -

- ing, they're talk - ing.
- ing, you're dy - ing.
- est, the great - est, the great - est.

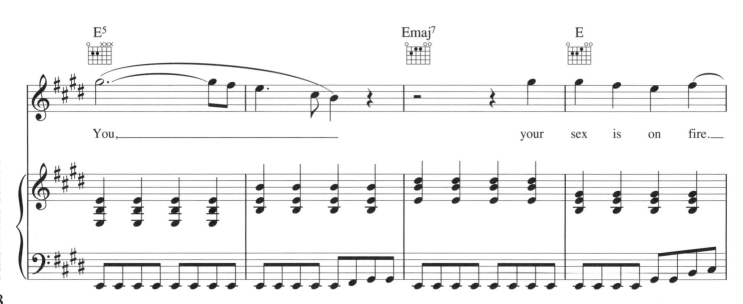

You,_____ your sex is on fire.__

E5
Emaj7
E
You, your sex is on fire.
C♯m7
4fr
Amaj9
Con-sumed
E5
Emaj7
E
with what's to trans - pire.
C♯m7
4fr
Amaj9
E

Technical Exercises

Group A: Scales

The blues scale should be prepared as shown below. You may select any starting note from A–E. You will be asked if you would like to sing along to a metronome click or hear four clicks before you start. Whichever option you choose, you will hear your chosen starting note before the count starts. You may perform this test using any vocal sound except humming or whistling. The tempo is ♩=100.

Group B: Arpeggios

In this group, the arpeggio exercise needs to be prepared as shown below.

This test is performed to a metronome click track and you may select any starting note from C–G. You will hear the root note played on piano followed by a one-bar (four click) count-in. You may perform this test using any vocal sound except humming or whistling. The tempo is ♩=100.

C major arpeggio and C diminished arpeggio

Group C: Intervals

In this group, both the major and minor interval sequences need to be prepared as below. You will be asked to perform one of them in the exam, as chosen by the examiner.

The examiner will choose a starting note within the range D–F. You will hear this note followed by a four-beat count-in. You may perform this test using any vocal sound except humming or whistling. The tempo is ♩=90.

Major 7th and major 6th intervals

Minor 7th and minor 6th intervals

Group D: Backing Vocals

In this group, all three backing vocal parts need to be prepared as shown below. You will be asked to perform one of them in the exam, as chosen by the examiner. The chosen part must be sung alongside the other two parts on the recording. The backing tracks for these can be found on the download card.

Group E: Stylistic Studies

You will need to choose *one* stylistic technical study from the group listed below and perform it to the backing track, a copy of which can be found on the download card. Your choice of style will determine the style of the Quick Study Piece. If you choose the jazz and blues stylistic study, for example, the examiner will give you a QSP from the jazz and blues group.

- Pop and musical theatre
- Soul and R'n'B
- Jazz and blues
- Rock and indie

Stylistic Study | Pop and Musical Theatre

Even note slides / Melismas

Stylistic Study | Soul and R'n'B

Rapid note bends in held notes / Speak-rap-patter phrasing

Stylistic Study | Jazz and Blues

Scat singing / Smooth phrasing with gentle bends

As I walked down your street___ last night,___

I could hear the rhy - thm of my beat - ing heart.___ You set me on fire___

___ with your ski - pi - dy do wah wah a - dip - de woo woo.
(Students may use their own adlib/scats here as an alternative)

I feel your car - res - ses___ send - ing shi - vers___ down my spine.

Stylistic Study | Rock and Indie

Trill downs / Registration flips

You've found your place in the world,___ but your

head's in a diff'-rent space. Take your time to look a - round___ or you may lose your___ way.

Get your head out of the clouds,___ be - fore you lose this re - a - li - ty.___ Look

down from your i - v'ry tow - er, and see me walk a - way.___

Quick Study Piece

At this grade you will be asked to prepare and perform a short Quick Study Piece (QSP). This will consist of four bars of melody and eight bars of improvisation. Bars 1–4 of the test will be a notated melody and you will need to sing all the written detail, including lyrics. In bars 5–8 you will need to improvise a variation of bars 1–4, developing both the lyrics and melody as you feel appropriate. In bars 9–12 you will need to improvise with no requirement to reference bars 1–4. You may use any vocal sound except humming or whistling for these bars.

The examiner will give you the sheet music, then you will hear a full mix version of the track, including the notated parts. This first playthrough will be preceded by the root note and a one-bar count-in. After the full mix, you will have three minutes to practise. The root note will be played at the start of this practice time and then again after 90 seconds. During the practice time, you will be given the choice of a metronome click throughout or a one-bar count-in at the beginning.

At the end of three minutes, the backing track will be played twice more with the notated parts now absent. The first time is for you to rehearse and the second time is for you to perform the final version for the exam. Again, you will hear the root note and a one bar count-in before both playthroughs. The backing track is continuous, so once the first playthrough has finished, the root note and count-in of the second playthrough will start immediately. The tempo is ♩=70–160.

The QSP style will be from one of the following four groups. These match the groups of the stylistic studies in the Technical Exercises section.

- Pop and musical theatre
- Soul and R'n'B
- Jazz and blues
- Rock and indie

The style given to you in the exam will be from the same group as your choice of stylistic study. The examiner will decide which one, specifically.

Quick Study Piece | Pop and Musical Theatre   *Example test*

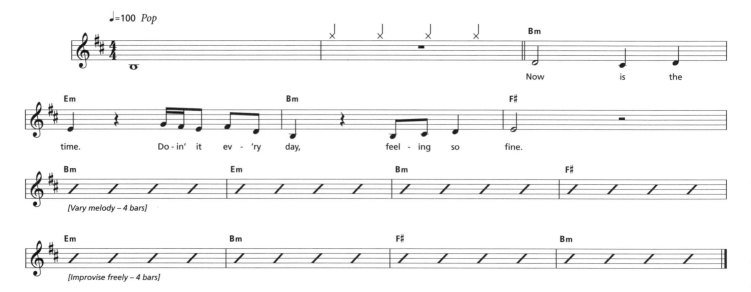

Quick Study Piece | Soul and R'n'B

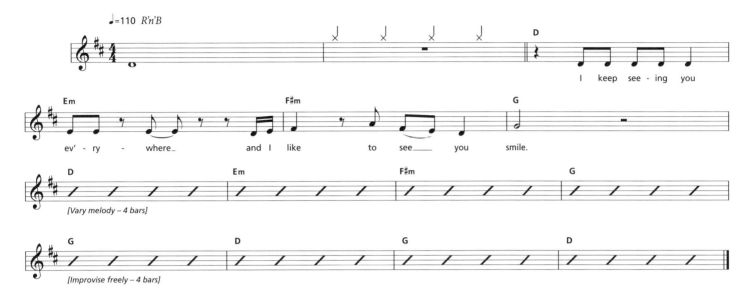

[Vary melody – 4 bars]

[Improvise freely – 4 bars]

Quick Study Piece | Jazz and Blues

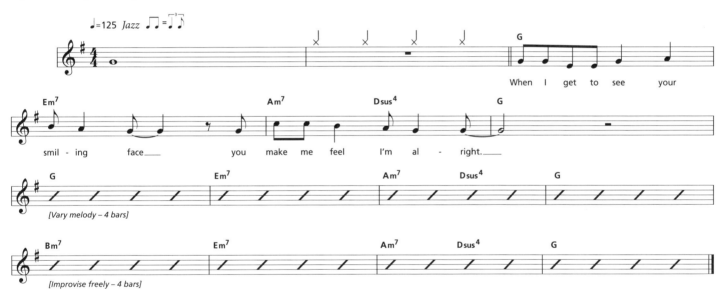

[Vary melody – 4 bars]

[Improvise freely – 4 bars]

Quick Study Piece | Rock and Indie

[Vary melody – 4 bars]

[Improvise freely – 4 bars]

Ear Tests

In this section, there are two ear tests:
- Melodic Recall
- Harmony Vocals

You will find one example of each type of test printed below and you will be given both of them in the exam.

Test 1 | Melodic Recall

The examiner will play you a two-bar melody played to a drum backing. It will use the E major or D natural minor scales (the examiner will decide which), and the first note will be the root note or the 5th. You will hear the test twice. Each time the test is played, it starts with the root note and a four-beat count-in. There will be a short gap for you to practise after each playthrough. Next, you will hear a *vocal* count-in, after which you should sing the melody to the drum backing. The tempo is ♩=90.

It is acceptable to sing over the track as it is being played as well as practising after the first two playthroughs. The length of time available after the second playthrough is pre-recorded on the audio track, so the vocal count-in may begin while you are still practising.

You may perform this test using any vocal sound except humming or whistling.

Please note: the test shown is an example. The examiner will give you a different version in the exam.

Test 2 | Harmony Vocals

The examiner will play you a four-bar melody in the key of G major or A major, based on the I–IV–V–VI chords. The recorded vocal part will sing the root, 3rd or 5th of each chord, and you need to harmonise a diatonic 3rd or 4th above this part using the same rhythm. The examiner will give you the lyrics.

You will hear the test twice. Each time the test is played, it starts with the root note and a four-beat count-in. There will be a short gap for you to practise after each playthrough. Next, you will hear a *vocal* count-in, after which you should perform the harmony line. The tempo is ♩=90–120.

It is acceptable to sing over the track as it is being played as well as practising after the first two playthroughs. The length of time available after the second playthrough is pre-recorded on the audio track, so the vocal count-in may begin while you are still practising.

Please note: the test shown is an example. The examiner will give you a different version in the exam.

General Musicianship Questions

In this part of the exam you will be asked five questions. Three of these will be about general music knowledge, the fourth will be about improvisation, and the fifth will be about your voice or the microphone.

Part 1 | General Music Knowledge

The examiner will ask three music knowledge questions from the categories below. The questions will be based on one of the pieces (including Free Choice Pieces) as performed by you in the exam. You can choose which one.

If there are handwritten notes on the piece you have chosen, the examiner may ask you to choose an alternative.

You will be asked to *identify and explain:*
- Any notation used in the chosen piece.
- Recognition of any interval up to an octave between two adjacent notes. (You will need to state major, minor or perfect.)

Part 2 | Improvisation

You will be asked to briefly *describe and demonstrate* – with reference to melody, rhythm, phrasing, dynamics and expression – your approach to how you would improvise any part of your chosen song. You can choose the part.

Part 3 | Your Voice And The Microphone

The examiner will also ask you one question about your voice or the microphone. They will decide which. Brief demonstrations to assist your answer are acceptable.

You will be asked:
- Name three effective resonators for singing.
- Explain the difference between 'aspirate onset' and 'glottal onset'.
- Which exercises might be safe to perform when your voice is tired or you have a sore throat?
- How can you balance your sound on microphone when switching between chest voice (low register) and head/falsetto voice (high register)?

Entering Exams, Exam Procedure & Marking Schemes

Entering Exams

Entering a Rockschool exam is easy. You can enter online at *www.rockschool.co.uk* or by downloading and filling in an exam entry form. The full Rockschool examination terms and conditions as well as exam periods and current fees are available from our website or by calling +44 (0)845 460 4747.

Exam procedure

In the exam you can decide whether to start with the Performance Pieces or the Technical Exercises. These will be followed by the Supporting Tests (Ear Tests and Quick Study Pieces) and General Musicianship Questions.

Use Of Microphone

At Level 1 (Grades 1–3) microphone use is optional, although candidates may use one if they feel it will enhance their performance. At Level 2 (Grades 4–5) microphone use is obligatory for all pieces and at Level 3 (Grades 6–8) for the whole exam.

Marking Schemes

Below are the marking schemes for the two different types of Rockschool exam.

Grade Exams | Grades 6–8

ELEMENT	PASS	MERIT	DISTINCTION
Performance Piece 1	12–14 out of 20	15–17 out of 20	18+ out of 20
Performance Piece 2	12–14 out of 20	15–17 out of 20	18+ out of 20
Performance Piece 3	12–14 out of 20	15–17 out of 20	18+ out of 20
Technical Exercises	9–10 out of 15	11–12 out of 15	13+ out of 15
Quick Study Piece	6 out of 10	7–8 out of 10	9+ out of 10
Ear Tests	6 out of 10	7–8 out of 10	9+ out of 10
General Musicianship Questions	3 out of 5	4 out of 5	5 out of 5
TOTAL MARKS	**60%+**	**74%+**	**90%+**

Performance Certificates | Grades 1–8

ELEMENT	PASS	MERIT	DISTINCTION
Performance Piece 1	12–14 out of 20	15–17 out of 20	18+ out of 20
Performance Piece 2	12–14 out of 20	15–17 out of 20	18+ out of 20
Performance Piece 3	12–14 out of 20	15–17 out of 20	18+ out of 20
Performance Piece 4	12–14 out of 20	15–17 out of 20	18+ out of 20
Performance Piece 5	12–14 out of 20	15–17 out of 20	18+ out of 20
TOTAL MARKS	**60%+**	**75%+**	**90%+**

Improvisation Requirements & Free Choice Pieces

At Rockschool it is our aim to encourage creativity and individualism. We therefore give candidates the opportunity to express themselves musically within styles of their own choice. For this reason, Free Choice Pieces are accepted in all Vocals grades. In addition, all songs performed in exams from Grade 3 onwards have compulsory improvisation requirements.

Improvisation Requirements

From Grade 3, all songs, whether from the grade book or chosen as FCPs, need to incorporate improvisation. The improvisation can be prepared in advance, but is expected to be individually constructed, and needs to include *both* vocal ad-libbing and re-working of existing melody lines as follows:

Level 1 Grade 3:	Vocal ad-libbing (2–4 bars) and re-working of melody line (4 bars)
Level 2 Grades 4–5:	Vocal ad-libbing (4–8 bars) and re-working of melody line (4–8 bars)
Level 3 Grades 6–7:	Vocal ad-libbing (8–12 bars) and re-working of melody line (8 bars)
Level 3 Grades 8:	Vocal ad-libbing (12–16 bars) and re-working of melody line (8 bars)

For all pieces, you will need to highlight the sheet music to show the examiner the location of both ad-libbed and re-worked parts at the beginning of the exam.

Notes

- You are free to choose where you improvise. However, in all cases, improvisations need to be a continuous number of bars, not a number of smaller bars which in total add up to the ranges shown.

- Vocal ad-lib could be demonstrated in, for example, introductions, endings or open instrumental parts.

- Re-working of a melody could be demonstrated by altering any existing singing parts; for example, verses, choruses, bridges.

- For both ad-lib and re-working of a melody, you need to demonstrate an awareness of harmony, melody, phrasing, use of rhythms and incorporation of any appropriate expression in a stylistically appropriate manner. Range and content will be expected to increase progressively as you move through the grades.

- We would encourage re-working to take place later in a piece after the original has been presented to show you can portray the original, then you are able to adapt appropriately with individual colour.

- Improvisation can be a good place to demonstrate your head voice, which can often be omitted, reducing the technical content of a piece at a particular grade.

Free Choice Pieces (FCPs)

An FCP is defined as any piece outside the grade book, and can fall into two categories:

1) **Wider Repertoire:** a full list of pre-approved and regularly updated pieces can be found on *www.rockschool.co.uk*. These songs can be used *without* prior approval from Rockschool.

2) **Own Choice:** candidates can choose any song in any genre outside the grade book and wider repertoire. These songs can, however, only be used *with* prior approval from Rockschool. This requirement is compulsory and you need to contact the office to have your chosen piece(s) approved. Please allow five weeks before your exam to receive a decision.

We cannot accept any songs which have not been approved or are not contained in the grade book or wider repertoire.

For all grades, candidates can choose the following number of FCPs in the exam:

Grade Examinations:	Up to 2 of 3 pieces can be free choice. (At least one piece must be from the grade book.)
Performance Certificates:	Up to 3 of 5 pieces can be free choice. (At least two pieces must be from the grade book.)

For all FCPs, candidates will need to bring the sheet music and a backing track (without vocal part) on the day. A memory stick, iPod or CD/DVD is acceptable and we would also suggest a second source to be safe. It will not be necessary to bring the sheet music or backing tracks for pieces chosen from the grade book.

Copyright Information

Ain't No Sunshine
(Withers)
Universal/MCA Music Limited

Counting Stars
(Tedder)
Sony/ATV Music Publishing (UK) Limited

I Can't Quit You Baby
(Dixon)
Bug Music Limited/Jewel Music Publishing Company Limited

Jealousy
(Young/Eliot/Stilwell)
Sony/ATV Music Publishing (UK) Limited

Man In The Mirror
(Ballard/Garrett)
Universal/MCA Music Limited/BMG Rights Management (UK) Limited

Sex On Fire
(Followill/Followill/Followill/Followill)
Warner/Chappell Music Limited/Bug Music (Windswept Account)/Bug Music Ltd

mcps